MICHAEL COLLINS

**Discover history's heroes
and their stories:**

Ida B. Wells

DISCOVERING HISTORY'S HEROES

HEROES

MICHAEL COLLINS

BY JAMES BUCKLEY JR.

Aladdin

New York   London   Toronto   Sydney   New Delhi

ALADDIN

An imprint of Simon & Schuster Children's Publishing Division

1230 Avenue of the Americas, New York, New York 10020

First Aladdin hardcover edition August 2019

Text copyright © 2019 by James Buckley, Jr.

Jacket illustration copyright © 2019 by Lisa K. Weber

Also available in an Aladdin paperback edition.

For information about special discounts for bulk purchases,

please contact Simon & Schuster Special Sales at

1-866-506-1949 or business@simonandschuster.com.

The Simon & Schuster Speakers Bureau can bring authors to your live event.

For more information or to book an event contact the Simon & Schuster Speakers

Bureau at 1-866-248-3049 or visit our website at www.simonspeakers.com.

Jacket designed by Nina Simoneaux

Interior designed by Mike Rosamilia

The text of this book was set in Adobe Caslon Pro.

Manufactured in the United States of America 0719 FFG

2 4 6 8 10 9 7 5 3 1

Library of Congress Cataloging-in-Publication Data

Names: Buckley, James, Jr., 1963- author.

Title: Michael Collins : discovering history's heroes / by James Buckley Jr.

Description: New York : Jeter Publishing, 2018. | Audience: Ages 7-10.

Identifiers: LCCN 2018019225 (print) | LCCN 2018022405 (eBook) |

ISBN 9781534424807 (hc) | ISBN 9781534424791 (pbk) |

ISBN 9781534424814 (eBook)

Subjects: LCSH: Collins, Michael, 1930—Juvenile literature. | Space flight to the
moon—Juvenile literature. | Project Apollo (U.S.)—Juvenile literature. | Astronauts—
United States—Biography—Juvenile literature.

Classification: LCC TL789.85.C65 (eBook) |

LCC TL789.85.C65 B83 2018 (print) | DDC 629.450092 [B]—dc23

LC record available at https://lccn.loc.gov/2018019225

On being alone on the far side of the moon:
I feel this [feeling] powerfully—not as fear
or loneliness—but as awareness, anticipation,
satisfaction, confidence, almost exultation.
–Michael Collins, *Carrying the Fire*

Heroes abound, and should be revered as such,
but don't count astronauts among them. We work
very hard; we did our jobs to near perfection, but
that was what we had hired on to do.
–Michael Collins, 2009 NASA statement

CONTENTS

Introduction   **Another Hero**   1

Chapter 1   **A Young World Traveler**   5

Chapter 2   **Learning to Fly**   11

Chapter 3   **A Test Pilot**   20

Chapter 4   **Choosing Astronauts**   25

Chapter 5   **Early Days at NASA**   31

Chapter 6   **Iguanas and Rocks**   36

Chapter 7   **Space Tailor**   40

Chapter 8   **First Crew Assignment**   45

Chapter 9   ***Gemini 10*!**   50

Chapter 10   **Finally in Space**   55

Chapter 11   **A Walk in Space**   63

Chapter 12   **Coming Home, Part 1**   69

Chapter 13   **Disaster!**   73

Chapter 14   **Preparing for the Moon**   80

Chapter 15   **Patches and Packing**   87

Chapter 16   **Liftoff!**   94

Chapter 17   **A Three-Day Trip**   98

Chapter 18 **On the Moon**   102

Chapter 19 **Alone**   105

Chapter 20 **The Most Important Job of All**   109

Chapter 21 **Coming Home, Part 2**   114

Chapter 22 **Around the World Again**   122

Chapter 23 **His Next Big Job**   128

Chapter 24 **A Private Life . . . Mostly**   134

            Endnotes   139

            Bibliography   141

MICHAEL COLLINS

Introduction
ANOTHER HERO

Glance up into the sky from just about anywhere on Earth (as long as it's nighttime, and as long as it's not too cloudy) . . . and you can see the moon. This giant space rock has been spinning around Earth for 4.5 billion years or so. Human beings like you have been looking up at the moon for only about 300,000 of those years. That's still a pretty long time.

For 299,950 of those years, staring up at the moon was all any of us could ever do. Flying up there and standing on it? The stuff of dreams.

... until those dreams came true on July 20, 1969—that day, two members of our species climbed out of a metal contraption and stood on the moon. Those two astronauts—Neil Armstrong and Edwin "Buzz" Aldrin—instantly became world famous. For all of history, they will always be the first men on the moon. Their courage was cheered from America to Timbuktu. They became heroes.

However, another human being was up there too. Michael Collins didn't get to walk on the moon, but without him the other two heroes would not have come back. That first mission to the moon, *Apollo 11*, was a three-person job ... this book is about person number three, who in our eyes is just as much a hero as the other two gents.

Of course, Collins has said over and over again that he doesn't think he's a hero. Lots of heroes say that, actually. It's one of the things that unite them as heroes. They usually don't think what they're doing is really special. They think that they're just doing a job that needs to be done. But we believe that celebrating such people is important. By learning more about the heroes who have not been in the spotlight, we can know more about our history. We can see how we arrived at this point and, perhaps more important, how we can form our future.

The *Apollo 11* trip was actually the second into space for Collins, after a career as a daring test pilot. On an earlier mission for the National Aeronautics and Space Administration (NASA), he was one of the first people to "walk" in space. He helped improve the special suits worn by Apollo astronauts. After his time as an astronaut, he led the drive to create one of the most popular museums in the world.

When you think about it, Michael Collins has lived such a full and amazing life that he would have been a hero even if he had never left Earth. Number three? How about number one?

1.
A YOUNG WORLD TRAVELER

When he was a kid, Michael Collins didn't grow up wanting to be an astronaut. There was a good reason for that. There were no astronauts when he was a kid. In fact, the first airplane had flown just twenty-seven years before his birth. When he was born, flying to the moon was something you read about in science fiction. It was not something you thought could be your job.

Later in his life, Collins did fly around the world, in more ways than one. He was born on Halloween,

October 31, 1930, in Rome, Italy. That didn't make him Italian, though. His father, Major General James Lawton Collins, was an officer in the United States Army. He had been one since before World War I. One of his first assignments had been to help the famous General John "Black Jack" Pershing chase down a Mexican bandit called Pancho Villa. James Collins then served in World War I. As Collins rose through the military ranks, the army sent him to different posts around the world. His family went along with him. Michael was very young when his family left Italy. They moved to Oklahoma first, then soon moved again, this time to New York City. Military families in the city lived on Governors Island. Michael could see the Statue of Liberty from there, as well as the skyscrapers of Manhattan.

Next stop was San Antonio, Texas. It was in Texas that Michael says he first started loving airplanes. He would sit and watch them take off and land at a small airfield near his house. He wondered what it would be like to be up there in the sky. He also started building model airplanes. His first was a one-seat racing airplane called a Gee Bee. He also enjoyed reading science fiction. "I was a big Buck Rogers fan and I used to prowl around in the caverns of Mongo," the planet that was the scene of many of the fictional Rogers's adventures.[1]

In 1940, General Collins became the head of army forces in Puerto Rico. The Collins family was on the move again. Michael loved his exotic new home. His family lived in a building called Casa Blanca, which means "White House." This large white home was one of the oldest buildings in the Americas. People had lived in it since 1530!

Puerto Rico amazed Michael. There he saw animals such as lizards and tropical fish. His house had a huge garden, too, filled with wild green plants. He also learned tough lessons when he ate local foods that did not agree with his American stomach.

In Puerto Rico the airplane-loving boy finally got

to ride in the sky. He and his father got a ride in a Grumman Widgeon. (A widgeon is a type of duck.) Michael got to sit in the copilot's seat and even steered the plane for a few moments. It was a thrill, and one he looked forward to repeating.

In 1941 the United States entered World War II. The army needed experienced officers to help run the war. General Collins was called to work in Washington, DC, at the Pentagon. That's the headquarters of the US armed forces. The Collins family left beautiful Puerto Rico behind and once again followed General Collins as he served his country. Michael's father wasn't the only one in the family to serve his country in this way. Michael's older brother, James, was by then a cadet at West Point, the United States Military Academy; and General Collins's brother Joseph was one of the senior commanders in Europe during World War II. Michael also had two sisters, Virginia and Agnes. The family lived in Virginia, outside DC.

Michael attended high school at St. Albans, a small private school. He was a good math student and was also on the wrestling team. He was not a big teenager, more on the skinny side. But he loved the action of sports and played on the offensive line for the football team.

After high school there was really only one place that Michael wanted to go. He wanted to continue a family tradition and serve his country. His good grades and family connections helped earn him an appointment to West Point.

The US Military Academy

America trains its army officers at this school in West Point, New York. The school first opened in 1802 on the banks of the Hudson River. Students are called cadets and are actually junior army officers when they start school. They study science, literature, and math but also military history and leadership.

When they graduate, they have to serve at least five years in the military.

Many of America's most famous generals studied there. Civil War generals Ulysses S. Grant of the Union army and Robert E. Lee of the Confederate army both graduated from West Point. General John Pershing led the US forces in World War I, and General Dwight D. Eisenhower led Allied forces in World War II. Both men attended West Point.

Other branches of the military have their own schools. The US Naval Academy is in Annapolis, Maryland. The US Air Force Academy is in Colorado Springs, Colorado. And the US Coast Guard Academy is in New London, Connecticut.

2.
LEARNING TO FLY

Michael joined the West Point Corps of Cadets in 1948. For his first year, as a freshman, he was called a plebe. The first-year students did lots of marching and had to follow orders from older students. West Point students, all men at the time, took classes in math, science, and literature, like most college students. They also studied military tactics. That is, they learned the skills they would need to lead men in combat. Michael has never said much about his time at West Point. His grades at graduation put him just outside the top third of his class, though. And then he had a decision to make.

At this time, in 1952, the US Air Force was still fairly new. It had grown out of a part of the army that flew planes and that had fought so well in World War II. In the new jet age after the war, the country needed a separate fighting force in the air. The Air Force Academy, however, did not open until 1954. To get officers for the new air force, the Pentagon allowed some West Point grads to join the new service. Collins remembered his youthful love of airplanes. He also realized that some people in the army might think he was getting special treatment. By now his uncle Joe was the army chief of staff, basically the boss of the entire army. Michael's father had retired as a two-star general. His brother had become a colonel, and two cousins were high-ranking officers. Michael loved the army, but he realized he had another way to serve. He chose to join the US Air Force. It was his first step to becoming an astronaut, but he didn't know it at the time.

The US Air Force

The first airplane flew in 1903. The first military airplane came along just six years later. Airplanes have been a big part of the US armed forces ever since. During World War I and until the end of World War II, airplanes were part of the army, and so the US Army Air Forces was created.

Following the war, a new branch just for airplanes was born. The US Air Force came into being in 1947. Today it has bases all over the world and flies everything from small propeller planes to enormous cargo craft. The service's most famous airplane is *Air Force One*, used only by the president of the United States.

In fact, Michael almost never made it into the pilot's seat. To enter the air force's pilot-training program, he had to take medical tests. One of them checked his eyesight. The first time he took one of the eye tests, he flunked! But the doctors gave him a second chance. Like the good student he was, he got information on eye exercises and worked hard for a week. When he took the eye test again, he passed. Next stop: pilot school.

Michael took to flying like a fish takes to water. He learned in a single-engine plane called a T-6 Texan. The air force assigned him to bases in Mississippi and Texas. He is left-handed, and many flight controls use the pilot's right hand. But he practiced on the ground and in the air, and soon was soaring through the sky. He later flew in his first jet airplane, a T-33.

His success at that first pilot school led to a special new posting. In 1950 the United States had joined other countries in fighting the Korean War. That war was the first in which both sides had jet fighter airplanes. So Collins was sent to learn to fly these kinds of planes at Nellis Air Force Base in Las Vegas.

As he battled through the intense training, Collins began to realize more than ever the danger of his job. He was in Las Vegas for about three months. In that time, more than twenty pilots were killed in training accidents. Still, Michael kept flying. He was learning to pilot the air force's F-86 Sabrejet. It had room for one pilot and flew as fast as 690 miles per hour. It was designed to shoot guns at other fighter jets and to drop bombs on enemy targets. In training the student pilots zigged and zagged high above the empty desert. They learned to aim at enemy fighters but also to avoid them when being chased.

Michael avoided the accidents, learned his lessons, and became a fighter pilot. By the time he finished training, however, the Korean War had ended. So he began another winding path around the world. Just as he had done when he was a kid, he went wherever the US military sent him.

First he flew from a base in the Southern California

desert. Then, in 1954, he was assigned to a base in France. To get there the pilots hopscotched their planes in short flights from California to Europe.

It was not all beautiful flying, however. During one test flight in 1956, Collins nearly died. Something went wrong with the plane's engine. He got an alarm in the cockpit but was not sure what was happening. Then another pilot sent him a warning over the radio—his airplane was on fire! Michael was scared, but he knew what to do. He had trained over and over for emergencies. He grabbed a lever and popped off the plastic canopy over his head. Then he pulled another lever and held on tight. A huge blast sent him flying out of the plane, still strapped to his seat. A few seconds later he popped off the seat belt and flew freely. As he fell toward the ground, he pulled a metal ring on his vest, and a parachute popped open above him. He floated down to the ground and landed with a bump, but was unhurt.

Because of accidents like this one, pilots also had

to learn to survive on the ground. What if he had parachuted into a forest far from people? For one of his survival lessons, he hiked for ten days through tree-covered hills. He carried only a small amount of food and had to find more on the way. One of the items he was given was a live rabbit. (What did he do with it? "Don't ask," he writes.)[2]

In Europe he and his fellow pilots learned a new type of flying. At the US desert bases they had huge, empty skies to zoom around in. In Europe there was less room. They practiced flying closer to the land, hugging the low hills and diving into valleys. They did sometimes get to fly over North Africa, once again enjoying wide-open skies.

At a US base in Libya in 1956, Michael took part in a competition among fighter pilots from all over Europe. They battled in mock fights, took target practice, and showed off their flying skills. When the points were totaled, Michael had won one of the events! He writes that he treasures the trophy he won that day "above more prestigious honors that have since come my way."[3]

While in Europe, Michael gained something else that he would treasure. In 1956 he met Patricia Finnegan in France. She was from Boston and was working for a company in France. It was love at first sight. "When she walked into the room, it was like a thousand-watt light bulb went off. She just lit the place up," Collins once said. "She was smart, she was beautiful, she was very strong."[4] They were married in 1957.

So he was one of the air force's best pilots. But what else did he want to do? Michael's brother-in-law was a test pilot. The chance to try out new planes and fly in different situations sounded like a good idea to Michael. There was only one problem. To apply to become a test pilot, you had to have fifteen hundred hours of time flying jet aircraft. Michael had a lot, but not that much. So for the next three years, he took various jobs in the air force while trying to amass more hours at the controls of a jet. (One of those jobs took him to Boston, near his wife's family. He and Pat had Kate, their first child, in 1959.)

Finally, in 1960, as soon as Michael reached fifteen hundred hours, he applied to be a test pilot. He didn't think he would get in, even with his great record. He knew that all the best pilots wanted this important assignment. But in late August he got the letter he wanted. He was assigned to Test Pilot School at Edwards Air Force Base in Southern California. It was time to move again.

3.
A TEST PILOT

Being a military pilot is a dangerous job. Remember all those training accidents? And in combat, usually even more pilots crash or get hurt. Compared to being a test pilot, though, being a military pilot is easy. Being a test pilot is one of the most dangerous jobs a person can have.

New airplanes need to be tested before they are sent out to the militaries of the world. New airplanes don't always work just right, however. It is the job of test pilots to fly those new airplanes and make sure they work. If the aircraft don't work, it can mean disaster.

But that was a chance Michael was willing to take.

To learn how to do this job, Michael took flight after flight on jet airplanes. He studied for hours in classrooms, too. All those math classes he'd taken at West Point came in handy. Test pilots need to know everything about the science of flight and how airplanes work. During Test Pilot School, for each test flight Michael had to read dozens of reports. Then, after the flight, he had to study the data from the airplane. He would watch film of the flight and look at pictures, graphs, and charts of information. Then he had to write up a detailed report for his instructors.

The next day . . . time to do it all over again.

It was hard work, but it meant a chance to fly almost every day. Michael knew that he would have to work very hard to graduate from the school. He watched the actual test pilots zoom up in F-104 Starfighters. Those pilots wore shiny silver suits specially made to help them deal with the high speeds and altitudes. Michael was stuck in his canvas flight suit and couldn't wait to get out of it!

Finally, after more than nine months of classwork and endless reports, the grades came in. Many of the pilot students didn't make it. Others made it but were given jobs that probably meant lots more report-writing in their future. Out of all the students in his class, only one got offered a job at the air force's highest test pilot level—Fighter Ops. That one student was Michael Collins.

At Fighter Ops he was the new guy. At first he was given the most boring jobs. Boring to a test pilot, that is. Anyone else would have been scared silly! For several weeks he had to test something called the barrier. This was a machine that had a wire that could stop a runaway jet as it landed. The pilot dropped a hook from the back of the plane. The hook grabbed the wire. But the experts needed to make sure that this procedure worked no matter how fast the plane was traveling when it landed. So Michael had to drop the hook at the end of flight after flight.

While Michael had been learning to be a test pilot, other pilots had been looking farther ahead. In 1959 the United States had chosen seven men, all pilots, to become the first astronauts. In the late 1950s new rocket engines had allowed Russia to send a satellite into space. The United States then found itself in a "space race" with its Communist enemy. We needed brave men to ride those rockets, in an effort to keep up with the Russians. In fact, Russia's Yuri Gagarin became the first man in space in April 1961. From that first group of seven Mercury astronauts, as they were called, Alan Shepard became the first American in space in May 1961. For pilots like Michael, a new kind of flying was now possible. He suddenly could imagine flying not just jets but spacecraft. Men like him would be able to fly not just high in the sky but actually into space itself.

The space race heated up even more when President John F. Kennedy announced a bold goal—"to land a man on the moon and return him safely to Earth by the end of the decade." He said that in 1962. That gave the United States eight years. The space race was really on!

In 1962 another of those first seven astronauts, John Glenn, became the first man to orbit Earth. More flights were planned, and thus, more astronauts were needed. Only pilots were being considered, since flying was a big part of being an astronaut. Though testing the air force's new F-111 was an exciting challenge, Michael knew that he wanted to be part of this new adventure.

4.
CHOOSING ASTRONAUTS

The National Aeronautics and Space Administration (NASA) was the part of the US government that ran the space program. In 1962 it was time to pick more astronauts. Michael put his name into the hat right away. He was one of more than two hundred men who applied to become astronauts. (No women were allowed to apply. The first woman astronaut was not selected until 1978. Also, all the applications during Collins's time came from white men. Other races were not excluded. It was just that at that point, there were only a handful of experienced military pilots who were not white. In the future, people of many ethnic backgrounds became astronauts. In 1967, Major Robert Lawrence of the air force became the first African American chosen to be an astronaut. Sadly, he was killed in a flight accident later that year.)

First the air force had to agree to let Michael try for one of the astronaut positions. They wanted to make sure he had a good shot and would not embarrass the service. They interviewed him at length about his skills and his experience. They also made him practice giving speeches and answering questions. Being an astronaut was about more than just being a pilot. You had to become a face of the space program. Astronauts had quickly become American heroes. Everyone wanted to make sure that these new heroes could talk about their experiences as well as have them.

Other people talked to Michael to see if he could handle the pressure of being an astronaut. He passed those tests with flying colors. His job as a test pilot had trained him to be able to think clearly under intense pressure.

Astronauts had to be in top shape, too. It was a physical job. You had to be able to deal with the power of a spacecraft flight and to be able to move your body in zero gravity. The physical and medical tests took five days! They examined every inch of Michael's body, inside and out. They looked at his eyes and his ears. They measured everything in his blood. They poked and prodded and peered.

After all that, the three hundred applicants were reduced to a final group of thirty-two. Then it was time for even more tests and interviews. One of the meetings was with the men who were already astronauts. They grilled each applicant on their flight knowledge and what they knew about spaceflight already. The existing astronauts also wanted to get to know the potential recruits. After all, some of these new astronauts might be flying into space with them.

Finally the word came out. Michael Collins was . . . *not* an astronaut. He had not been picked. He was crushed. But he recovered quickly and decided he would apply again as soon as it was possible. (By then he had even more support at home. He and Pat now had three children. Ann had been born in 1961 and Michael Jr. in 1962.) To help his case, Michael left Fighter Ops and joined a new kind of school. The air force had seen that flying in space was going to be part of the future, so it created a school for some top pilots to learn more about spaceflight. The US Air Force Aerospace Research Pilot School sent Michael back into the classroom. He had to learn about flying in space, about the spacecraft that would be used, and about the science of both. He did get to keep flying, though, practicing in the F-104 Starfighter, which could go faster than the speed of sound! It could also fly to nearly ninety thousand feet, which was just below the edge of space. So close and yet so far. . . .

Michael resolved to get into even better shape for

next time, and he quit smoking. In those days smoking was much more common than today. People did not understand all the serious health risks. But it was clear to Michael that smoking was not a good idea for him. Quitting was hard, and it took him months, but he finally put cigarettes behind him for good.

Finally, in the summer of 1963, he got another chance. This time NASA was talking only to test pilots, so Michael's odds got even better. He went through the interviews again, but this time he felt he was among friends. Thanks in part to no longer smoking, he did better than he ever had on the physical tests. After all the tests, he went back to work at Edwards Air Force Base and waited. And waited.

Finally, on October 14, 1963, he got a call from Deke Slayton, head of NASA's astronaut program. Slayton said he wanted to hire Michael, if Michael still wanted the job. Michael was thrilled. *Of course* he wanted it!

Michael was one of fourteen men chosen to be

part of the third group of American astronauts. That made a total of thirty. In the coming years some of them would become world famous, others would die, and some would simply do their jobs quietly and professionally.

Michael was thrilled with his new mission. He gathered Pat and their "crew" of three children and moved to Houston.

Next stop . . . space.

5.
EARLY DAYS AT NASA

Well, not exactly the *next* stop. Collins had a lot of work to do before he would set foot on a spacecraft.

First it was time to go back to school. The fourteen men chosen to be new astronauts had a lot to learn. They might all be ace pilots, but flying in space was a whole new ball game.

Michael started off with a set of more than 240 hours of classes. He studied astronomy and how rockets worked. He learned about predicting weather. He began to work on computers, which were still fairly new at the time. He learned how the different NASA spacecraft communicated.

He still got to fly, though. Some of the classes the men took were not in Houston. Collins and the other astronauts got to fly themselves around the country to take classes. They also visited labs and companies that were building components of the spacecraft. He was now part of an enormous plan. Since President Kennedy had announced his proposal in 1962, all of NASA had one goal: get to the moon.

The first missions, part of Project Mercury, had been just to see if spacecraft worked. The astronauts also learned how to orbit a spacecraft around Earth. With the Project Gemini missions, different systems would be tested with each mission. On some, scientists would study how the astronauts lived in space. Other missions tested takeoffs and landings. Others were designed to practice connecting up with other spacecraft. Step-by-step the missions built the way to the moon.

Each Gemini mission would have two astronauts. The crews were chosen by Deke Slayton, head of the astronaut corps. Michael watched as crew after crew was made up . . . and he was not in one.

After the Gemini flights were over, the Apollo flights would take further steps toward landing on the moon. At this point no one knew who would be on that moon flight. Michael was sure hoping it would be him.

Names from Myth

The three main NASA space programs in the 1960s were named for Greek or Roman gods. Mercury was the messenger of the gods. His winged feet made him super-fast. Of course, the planet nearest the sun is also named for him. The NASA Gemini program took its name from the fact that its ships carried two astronauts. "Gemini" is the name of a constellation of stars named for Castor and Pollux, twins of Greek myth. Two twins . . . two astronauts.

Apollo is the Greek god of the sun. He was considered one of the most important Greek gods. His significance in mythology made his name a good choice for NASA's biggest leap into space.

Along with learning how to fly the spacecraft, NASA was learning how to protect astronauts.

As the TV show *Star Trek* said, "Space . . . the final frontier." Any time people reach a frontier, they face new challenges. As Collins and the people at NASA looked at space, they saw challenges all over the place. They also saw danger. Much of the work of Project Gemini was looking at how to keep astronauts safe in space.

There was a lot that the scientists did not know. How long could a person live without gravity? Would their lungs and heart work the same way? How would all the gear work in the cold of space? How much fuel did the spacecraft need? Would radiation in space harm the astronauts? Would moondust poison them?

When falling back to Earth, would the pressure of landing hurt them?

Michael, the other astronauts, and NASA had a lot of work to do.

6.
IGUANAS
AND ROCKS

While many programs at NASA looked up, others looked down. That is, they looked at what happens after the spacecraft comes back to Earth.

Unlike an airplane, you can't steer a spacecraft—at least the ones they used in the 1960s. (The space shuttles that flew from 1981 to 2011 could land like airplanes, but the Gemini and Apollo vehicles could not.) The idea was that after reentry, each Gemini and Apollo spacecraft would land in the ocean. It would float there until a nearby navy ship picked it up. However, NASA always wanted to be ready for anything that might go wrong. So astronauts had to train to survive in all sorts of places.

Because of the way the spacecraft would be landing, NASA knew that it was possible that the craft could land in a jungle or a desert. So Michael and the others found themselves training in some very interesting places!

Their first stop was Panama. This Central American country has a large area of rain forest. Collins and fellow astronaut Bill Anders were dropped there by helicopter. They had machetes (large knives) and a few supplies. They had to hike through the dense, hot, wet jungle to their campsite. They quickly ran through their food. In camp they were bitten by bugs and got little sleep. The next morning they tried to fish in a stream and caught nothing. They tried to eat part of a palm tree, but it was rotten inside. Finally their survival teachers took pity on them and gave them an iguana to eat.

This was a real test. Could the brave astronauts kill, boil, and eat this large lizard? It turned out that Anders decided he was not hungry. Michael was, and he happily gulped down chunks of iguana meat.

The next day they were taken to meet some Chocós, local native people. Michael tried to explain to the Chocó chief that the Americans were training in the jungle so that they would be able to fly to the moon.[5] Finally, after battling more tiny insects called chiggers, the men climbed into a small raft. They headed up a river to meet a larger boat. At last . . . freedom from the jungle!

But that was not the end of their survival training. Next, Michael and astronaut Charlie Bassett were put in the desert near Reno, Nevada. The men used the cloth from their parachutes to make lightweight clothing. This protected them from the hot sun better than their heavy flight suits would have. They took a short hike. Then they dug a resting place in the hillside to escape some of the heat. This time around the training lasted only a day or so.

Michael and the other astronauts had one more important land journey before they started their space-flights. One of the subjects they had to study was geology. That's the study of rocks and minerals. The moon, of course, is a giant rock. NASA felt that any astronauts who might land there should know a lot about rocks.

After studying hundreds of rock samples in class, the men headed to the Grand Canyon to see rocks in place. The astronauts hiked down into the mighty canyon. They learned about the layers of rock and used picks to choose samples. For one part of the trip, Michael rode a burro. But Michael did enjoy this trip, though he said he liked the plants, the views, and the animals more than the rocks.

The men also went to Meteor Crater in Arizona, an extinct volcano in New Mexico, and a lava bed in Oregon. Was any of this like the moon? It would be a few years before they really found out.

7.
SPACE TAILOR

After the classroom work wrapped up, each of the fourteen new astronauts was given a special job. That is, they became responsible for one part of the mission. They would have to learn all parts of the mission, but one part would be their main focus.

Michael did not feel that his math and science skills were as honed as other astronauts'. So he chose to work on the pressure suits. That was what all the astronauts would wear in the spacecraft. They also wore helmets during liftoff and space walks. (Astronauts call space walks "extravehicular activity," or EVA.)

Pressure suits—they did not call them "space suits"—protected the astronauts. On Earth the atmosphere creates pressure that lets us breathe safely. In space that pressure is almost gone, so breathing is impossible. Of course, there's no air in space either! The spacesuits created pressure close to the astronauts so they could breathe the pumped-in oxygen. Under the suits, the astronauts wore a thin cloth layer. In that layer, water flowed through tubes to help the astronauts stay cool. The inner layer was also stretchy. Astronauts have to do lots of jobs. The suit had to allow them to handle any task.

The outside of the suit had to be thick, to protect the men from the cold of space. It also had to be tough. When the astronauts were outside the spacecraft, they were sometimes hit by micrometeorites, which are super-tiny bits of rock, dust, or even man-made space junk. Even a tiny speck can do damage when moving at superfast speeds. The outer layer of the pressure suit needed to help stop those projectiles.

The helmets sealed in air too, of course. They also had radios. A special visor could be pulled down, sort of like a sun shade. The strength of the sun in space is much greater than on Earth. Gemini and Apollo helmets had sun shields that were gold plated!

As he did with everything he took on, Michael jumped into his new job with both feet. He met with the suit's makers. Different companies made different parts of the suits. So he traveled, learned, and helped. Mostly he learned. Lots of experts had a say in how the pressure suits would work. But Michael was one of the men who would wear them . . . and he would need it to keep him alive. For himself and his fellow astronauts, he had to be focused! It would be his job to test all the possible suit designs. All the sample suits, he wrote, came in one size: "Mike Collins."

He tried them on, one at a time, and took them through all sorts of tests. To see how the suits would do without gravity—which would be the conditions in space—he took flights on a special airplane.

The KC-135 cargo plane had a huge open area behind the cockpit. Imagine a jet airliner without seats. The pilot of these planes would fly almost straight up and then dive back down. For twenty seconds at the top of that flight, anyone inside would feel weightless. They would float! During that short time, Michael and others, wearing their suits and helmets, did tasks that they would do in space. He learned how to move in zero gravity. He learned how the suit needed to be fixed to work better. He saw which helmets fit best and which gloves let him move his fingers.

The plane would make the up-and-down loop over and over.

An experienced pilot like Michael had no trouble on these flights. For others, however, the movement was a bit tougher. The up-and-down motion created a lot of upset stomachs. Cameramen and engineers who were on the flight to observe Michael sometimes got sick. The KC-135's nickname? The Vomit Comet.

He also took the suits into a machine the men called "the wheel." You know how you feel on a merry-go-round? You feel the wind in your face, but you also feel a little pressure on your body as you go faster and faster. Astronauts on a rocket ship feel that pressure . . . times ten! Taking practice rocket rides wasn't possible, so Michael climbed into "the wheel." He sat in a tiny cab at the end of a long metal arm. The arm then spun around and around like an insane carnival ride. Faster and faster it went until Michael was feeling 10-g (that's how the force of gravity is measured). He could barely breathe! He had trouble seeing, and he almost blacked out. But the suits worked!

8.
FIRST CREW ASSIGNMENT

By the middle of 1965 the Gemini program was flying high. Several flights had been made, and the spacecraft were performing well. During the *Gemini 4* mission, Ed White became the first American to walk in space.

In June, Michael got his first official crew assignment. He and Ed White would be the backup crew for *Gemini 7*. That meant that his days of testing suits were over. It was time to train for a mission. He and White would be needed only if the main crew,

Frank Borman and Jim Lovell, got sick or injured. But the backup crew had to do all the same training, just in case.

For the next several months Michael and Ed White went step-by-step over the mission plan. *Gemini 7* would stay in space for fourteen days, to see how well human bodies could handle being weightless for that long. The astronauts would also practice linking up with another spacecraft. These procedures would be an important part of the moon landings, so NASA wanted to try them close to home.

The mission would also include medical experiments. Michael had to learn how to do all of them. Scientists wanted to see how human hearts would work without gravity for that long. Did hearts need gravity to beat? How about breathing? If the cockpit was kept pressurized, would that be enough? The astronauts didn't want to have to wear their helmets all the time, so finding that out was key. There was so much to learn.

As for flying the ship, there was not that much to do. Michael was an expert pilot, one of the best around. A pilot could do little in a spaceship, however. The astronauts joked that they were "canned man," like canned tuna. They were stuck in a tiny craft on top of a rocket. Once in space, they were in orbit, moving around without any engines or rockets needed.

During his training, Michael learned an important lesson: how to pee in space. Astronauts had to learn a twenty-step process. It involved tubes and bags and clips. Only one of the steps was actually peeing!

The *Gemini 7* flight was scheduled for December 4, 1965. By then Michael and Ed White were ready to fly. But so were Lovell and Borman. Michael's months of training didn't matter. On launch day he was just an observer.

More crew assignments were made, but Michael's name was not called. For the *Gemini 8* mission, he served an important role, however. He helped another astronaut family.

During that flight something went slightly wrong. Neil Armstrong and Dave Scott were aboard the craft. After connecting to an orbiting machine, their craft started to spin. Round and round it went, tumbling out of control. Finally Armstrong was able to shut off a thruster that was firing by mistake. "They were the hairiest ten minutes in the space program so far," Collins wrote later.[6]

As everyone watched and listened from far below, the astronauts jumped in to help. Michael went to Dave Scott's house to help take care of his kids. The media were very interested in every spaceflight. They wanted to have all the details of everything, from the astronaut's families to what the astronauts ate for dinner. So Michael knew that if something went really wrong, the Scott family would need help. He helped the kids and other family members avoid the gathered reporters. Things turned out fine, but it was a wake-up call for everyone. Spaceflight could be a dangerous business. The astronauts had to prepare for the worst as well as the best.

Soon after, Michael got the news he had been waiting for. Along with astronaut John Young, he had been assigned to *Gemini 10*!

Michael Collins was going to space!

9.
GEMINI 10!

Michael was overjoyed. He wrote that he didn't care how he got up to space, that he would fly with a kangaroo if he had to! But after celebrating his assignment, it was time to get to work.

When Michael and John Young heard the plan for *Gemini 10*, they worried about whether they could accomplish all of the tasks.

NASA had assigned fifteen scientific experiments to the flight. The astronauts would be taking pictures, measuring stars, and helping count micrometeorites. They would also be linking up to two other orbiting spacecraft. Finally, they would make two EVAs. Oh, yes . . . and they had to do all of that in three days! With a flight scheduled for July 1966, they got right to work.

Michael was very organized. He created a notebook with all the things he would have to learn and study for the mission. As each task was completed, he crossed it off his list—all 138 items.

After learning about the experiments, the men began practicing what they would do during the mission. To do this they "flew" in a machine called a simulator. This was a full model of a Gemini spacecraft. (A lot of people called the Gemini spacecraft "capsules." Michael and other astronauts disliked that term. A capsule is something you swallow, like a pill. You fly a spacecraft! Okay, sir. We'll say "craft"!) In the simulator the men could practice all the steps and tasks over and over. Making a mistake in the simulator was a way to learn. Making a mistake in space was a way to not come home.

Michael also got to see just how small the crew cockpit was. In the Gemini craft the two astronauts were crammed in like sardines. They basically never left their seats except to make space walks. He would be in there for almost four days on the flight, so learning how to feel comfortable was important.

The simulator was in St. Louis, so Michael was away from home often. He got a lot of support from Pat, who took care of the kids and the house. Michael usually got to spend Sundays at home, though. He looked forward to working around the house and taking care of his rose garden. He also tried to cook, but he said he was a better pilot than a cook!

Michael was selected to perform the EVA, so he had other training to do. On a space walk the astronaut is just floating. He is connected by a long hose to the spacecraft. But it is very hard for them to control how they move or "fly." To help, NASA created a sort of gun that shot out bursts of nitrogen gas. When the astronaut shot the gun in one direction, he would move in the other direction.

In order to practice using the gas gun, Michael put on his full pressure suit and helmet, plus an oxygen backpack. Then he climbed onto a special floating pad. It was like an early version of a robot vacuum cleaner, and it looked like a giant floor polisher. Riding on the hovering machine, Michael slid over the ground sort of like he would move in space. Over and over he practiced with the nitrogen gun. He learned how much to shoot, and when and how to keep himself from spinning or going too fast.

He also spent a lot of time with a tennis ball. He wasn't playing, however. He knew that his hands would need to work very hard for a very long time in space. He had hundreds of dials to turn, switches to flip, and levers to move. He could not afford for his hands to cramp or be weak. So everywhere he went, he carried a tennis ball and squeezed it repeatedly.

Step-by-step Michael crossed off his 138 items. He and Young learned to work as a team, to be ready for any emergency. During this time Michael paused to consider the danger. More than anyone else, astronauts knew all the things that could go wrong in space. And Michael knew that humans are not perfect and that something could be done incorrectly, which could put him in danger. He admitted to the fear, but not to what he called "emotional" fear. That is, he knew that he could be afraid of what might happen. However, he also knew that he could control his emotions by relying on his team, his skills, and his training. Getting scared would not make the mission easier or safer. He also wrote that as pilot, he was probably more afraid of messing up and being embarrassed than of anything else!

He knew something up there could kill him, but he flew on like the brave pilot he was.

10.
FINALLY IN SPACE

After all of his years of flying around Earth's skies, Michael was about to fly beyond them.

On the day of the launch—July 18, 1966—Michael slept in until noon. He wasn't being lazy; he was adjusting his body clock. The flight would take off at 5:20 p.m. Florida time, launching from Cape Canaveral. Huge rocket platforms and tall buildings called gantries dotted the flat, swampy landscape. Two of the rocket platforms would be used in the *Gemini 10* launch. One would send an Agena craft into orbit. That launch happened successfully shortly before the rocket carrying Michael and John Young lifted off. The two men would also try to track down another Agena target vehicle that had been launched weeks earlier.

After a final phone call to Pat back in Houston, Michael climbed into the familiar pressure suit. It actually took several people to get Michael dressed. First he pulled on a tube and a kind of underwear that would collect his urine. There was no other way to pee in space. Then he pulled on a stretchy suit like long johns. He needed help with a zipper on the back. Then he stepped into the boots, which were already connected to the pants and lower body section. The upper body section was lowered by helpers onto his upraised arms and over his head. It connected to the lower body with snaps and tight seals.

Onto each hand went a very tight glove. Helpers pulled them on and clicked them into rings on each arm, again forming a tight seal.

The helmet came last, clicking into place. From

that point on, he writes, he felt like he was on his way. He would breathe only pure oxygen until the helmet came off back on Earth.

After a few moments of resting on giant armchairs, the two astronauts climbed into an elevator that carried them ninety feet up to the top of the gantry. They carried small suitcases that held their temporary oxygen supplies. They were helped into the spacecraft feetfirst. Assistants clipped an oxygen line to their space suits and took away the suitcases. The men were also clipped into their seats, and their radios were carefully checked.

The rocket fired up far below them. People standing miles away suddenly grabbed their cameras and binoculars as smoke started to come from the huge engine.

The countdown began, and the men could hear it in their helmet radio earpieces: five . . . four . . . three . . . two . . . one . . . Ignition! Liftoff!

The noise was deafening, even high atop the

rocket. The two men felt the craft leave the ground, but they didn't feel great speed—yet. They could feel the pressure pushing them into their seats, but they were not uncomfortable. They rattled and rocked as the huge engines made everything around them vibrate.

When they were fifty seconds into the flight, Michael let go of a metal ring he had been tightly clutching. This was a parachute tab, and up until that moment the astronauts might have been able to eject if something had gone wrong. From that point on, there was no ejection possible. They were on their way.

As they flew higher and higher, they went faster and faster. They were smashed down into their seats by the massive pressure. They felt as much as 7-g, which is seven times the force of gravity.

Even as he sped toward space, Michael was in such a good mood that he found time for a joke. The two men in the craft could hear all the chatter among

NASA workers on the ground. One voice called for a meeting in a room at Cape Canaveral. Michael radioed down that he'd have to miss it!

The speed increased as temporary sections of the rocket fell away. At one point a huge shower of red and yellow sparks flew past the astronauts' window. But it was no danger; it was just part of the plan.

Finally *Gemini 10* reached orbit and Michael felt true weightlessness. Oddly, the first thing he noticed was not how he felt but what he saw—little bits of the craft floating all around him inside the cockpit. He did take a moment to look out the window too. He saw "the most glorious spectacle of sea and sky I have ever witnessed."[7]

But there was no time to be a tourist—it was time to go to work.

Cape Canaveral

Almost all of America's flights into space left Earth from Florida.

In the late 1940s the US military needed

a huge space to test new missiles. The base needed to be safely far from people, plus be near an ocean to allow test flights to land in the ocean. The site they chose was Cape Canaveral, a large area of swampland in southern Florida, home to more alligators than people. It was also the site of a Coast Guard lighthouse, so the government already owned much of the land. The good news was that there were roads and rail tracks already in place.

For more than a decade, missiles were launched from the site. When NASA began aiming rockets even higher, the facility proved to be just the right spot. All of the Mercury, Gemini, and Apollo missions launched from there. In 1963 the space center at Cape Canaveral was renamed to honor President John F. Kennedy, after he was assassinated. Kennedy was the leader who first urged Americans to fly to the moon.

The *Gemini 10* crew's first task was to make sure they knew where they were. Michael used an old-time instrument called a sextant to measure the distance between certain stars. He calculated angles between Earth and the sun and other stars. Then he did some math to get an answer. Meanwhile the computer instruments did the same calculation. This was to determine whether or not an astronaut could find the spacecraft's place without computer help, just in case. The computer was more accurate than Michael, but he was pretty close!

Knowing where they were was important, since their key task was to chase down the first Agena craft that had been launched before. They had to guide their craft using tiny thrusts into an orbit that would move them into a parallel path with the Agena. The Agena would also fire its thrusters to help with this delicate move.

But there was no time to celebrate. The two men guided their craft to get into the same orbit as the target vehicle, the Agena. Working carefully, they docked, or linked, the *Gemini* to the speeding Agena.

This was the first time that two spacecraft had connected while flying. As they linked up with the Agena, NASA informed them that they had now flown more than 475 miles above Earth, higher than any other humans in history! It was a key step toward a moon mission. There was much more work to do, however.

Having rocketed into space and worked hard for many hours, it was time for the men to rest. They placed metal plates over the windows to block the sun's rays, then strapped themselves in and tried to sleep. Michael found that his hands kept floating up away from his body. Finally he did some wedging and wiggling and found a way to sleep.

The next day, if all went well, he would walk in space.

11.
A WALK
IN SPACE

As *Gemini 10* zoomed along at an amazing 17,500 miles per hour, the two men did not feel as if they were going that fast. With no air or atmosphere to push against, the spacecraft did not feel like it was moving very much at all. Only the sight of Earth rushing by beneath them gave them a sense of movement.

Soon Michael would have a very different sense of motion.

With John Young's help, Michael connected his space suit to several hoses and cables. He was about to open a hatch and didn't want to float away! Michael's job was to take some photographs with a specially designed camera that had to be used away from the craft's windows. The glass in the spacecraft's windows blocked the sun's dangerous rays from the astronauts. However, it also made taking certain photos impossible.

Once he was hooked up, the hatch was opened and Michael Collins emerged into space. His feet remained in the craft, but his head was in the stars. Oddly, the stars were not twinkling as we see them from Earth.

When we look at the night sky from Earth, the stars seem to twinkle and wink. That's because the atmosphere around us breaks up the light before it reaches our eyes, and makes the stars sparkle. In space there is no atmosphere. The starlight is as strong and steady as a lightbulb.

As Michael took his photos, he and Young both suddenly had a problem. The sun slowly came up ahead of them as they whizzed around Earth. Strangely, though protected by helmet visors, their eyes began to water terribly. For a few scary moments Michael could barely see. Young's eyes weren't much better. "I can't see a gosh-darn thing," Young said, too cheerfully for Michael.[8] Their vision cleared enough for them to get Michael back inside safely and to close the hatch. In time, they could see fine again. Both men thought that the reason for the problem was a chemical used to keep their visors from fogging up. Houston said it would look into the problem.

The next day was the real highlight of the *Gemini 10* mission. After a sleep period they moved on to the business of finding the second Agena. Some careful math and nice flying brought them zooming along right next to it. While Young flew their craft, Michael got hooked up for a real space walk. For the first time ever, an astronaut would move from one flying spacecraft to another.

Michael went over every one of the seventy different steps on his checklists. When he was ready and connected, he opened the hatch. This time he left the ship completely. He held on to parts of the outside of the craft so that he wouldn't float away. He was now an object orbiting Earth at more than seventeen thousand miles an hour!

You might think that here is where he would have stopped and gazed in wonder. Or he might have been afraid as he floated in space. Or he might have looked at Earth to find the United States or something.

But he did none of that. He was too busy.

For the first several minutes, he moved carefully around the craft. He had to work closely with Young to avoid small jets, called thrusters. Young was using little bursts of fuel to operate these. Each burst of a thruster helped Young keep the Gemini craft in perfect parallel with the Agena. However, being near a thruster when it went off might melt Michael's suit, so he had to make sure he was clear when Young shot one off. Michael also was working hard not to get tangled in the cords, tethers, and tubes connected to his suit. Finally, all that work with his space "gun" came in handy. When he had his cords all set, he used the gun to push himself through space toward the Agena target. It was hard work, keeping himself from spinning out of control. It took him several minutes and repeated shots of the gas gun, but he finally grabbed on to the Agena. He had successfully made the trip, which was a big part of their mission. Once there, he removed an experiment that was strapped to the outside of the Agena. It measured micrometeorites. He retrieved the small box and then returned to *Gemini 10*. It took many minutes of slow movements for him to make it back. Once again he had to avoid any thruster jets. Finally, after what seemed a long time but was actually only about twenty-five minutes, Michael was back inside the spacecraft.

There they had another problem. The many feet

of cable and tube were now all inside! Michael said it looked like the snake house at a zoo. It took a few more minutes, but they finally got it all cleaned up.

Michael later wrote that it was in the rest period after his second EVA that he was finally able to look around and below him. He marveled at the green and blue seas. He saw entire continents. He saw fires and thunderclouds below. He saw islands in the sea, and vast green forests. He even took time to read a poem by a fellow pilot, one who had never gotten the chance to do what Michael was doing but had imagined it in just the same way.

12.
COMING HOME, PART 1

The following day—the last day of the *Gemini 10* mission—passed quickly. Michael and John Young continued with a few experiments. They began packing up gear for the ride home. They finished the last of their food for breakfast.

They also continued a NASA tradition. At different spots around the globe, people at small radio relay stations had been working throughout the trip. The astronauts can't always talk to Houston, but they can contact each relay as they fly over it. Now, as the spacecraft passed over each of the relay stations one last time, the *Gemini 10* crew said thanks to all the people working in those remote spots. Those folks didn't get the glory of the big job in Houston, but their work was just as important.

Finally, with help from the computers, the men and the craft were ready for the long trip home. First step: fire retro-rockets. "Retro" means "backward." These rockets slow the forward movement of the craft. As the craft slows, it is grabbed by gravity. Then the rockets fire to push them down toward Earth. Gravity takes over, and they fall . . . more than four hundred thousand feet!

The rockets fired, and down they went. As the craft fell through the atmosphere, it got hotter and hotter. Michael saw red-hot bits of the heat shield fly by their windows. He watched as a tail of fire and debris built behind them. And for five tense minutes, they could not talk to the ground. The heat around the craft made using the radio impossible.

Finally they passed fully into the atmosphere. They could use the radio again. The ground staff told them that they were on target!

A few moments later they pushed some buttons, and three huge parachutes popped out of the top of the spacecraft. Their rush toward Earth slowed very quickly.

They floated down and splashed into the Atlantic Ocean, home from a trip to space. Navy divers from a nearby ship leaped into the water and put a sort of life raft around the craft. The divers then helped open the hatch, and Michael and John Young breathed fresh air for the first time in four days. Michael remembered noticing how hot and humid the outside air was compared to the dry air inside the spacecraft.

One at a time they were put into a special sling and pulled up into a helicopter. They were carried to the nearby USS *Guadalcanal* and welcomed by sailors and NASA officials. Michael was happy to finally get out of the large, bulky, hot space suit that he had helped design!

The mission was over. The only real bad news was that because of a lost camera, there were no photos of Michael's space walk. But he would always have the memories.

The Navy and NASA

During the 1960s and early 1970s, NASA kept dropping spacecraft into the ocean. It was up to the navy to fish them out.

At the end of each Mercury, Gemini, and Apollo spaceflight, the craft parachuted into the sea. Navy ships were positioned around the globe to react. Usually they were able to be very close and reached the astronauts quickly. Most spacecraft landed within a few miles of a ship.

13.
DISASTER!

Following *Gemini 10*, there were two more Gemini flights. In fact, *Gemini 11* broke *Gemini 10*'s altitude record (which of course would be set for good by the Apollo moon flights).

Michael, however, was moved into the Apollo Program. Apollo flights would build toward an actual moon landing. At the time, however, no one knew which flight that would be or who would be on it.

Michael's first job in the Apollo Program was with the command module. Just as *Gemini 10* had docked with the first Agena target vehicle, the Apollo spacecraft would work in the same way. A command module (CM) would fly three astronauts to the moon. Then two of them would get into a smaller, lunar module (LM). The two modules would separate. While the LM did its work on the lunar surface, the CM would orbit the moon. When the work was done, the LM would fly up, and the CM would dock with it . . . and then everyone would go home.

At least that was the plan. Putting it into operation would take several years and lots of hard work.

Michael's first job was to help make the command module perfect. He spent time in Southern California, St. Louis, and Houston working with engineers and scientists. He was once again the tester, as he had been with the suits. He spent many weeks getting in and out of the small CM as each part was tested. (He did get to hang out in a fancy TV lounge while he waited for the engineers to make adjustments, though, and he got to eat at the engineering company's restaurant.)

The Apollo crews were not assigned yet, but it became clear to Michael that his role would be to pilot the CM. That made his chances of walking on the moon very small. However, he was fine with that. He had joined NASA to fly, and now he would be flying higher and farther than anyone ever had.

He also got a chance to learn a new way to fly. The LM and CM worked more like helicopters than like airplanes. So he went through "chopper" training. He learned to land the whirling machines on fields of rocks and dirt in California. This terrain was similar to the surface of the moon.

Sadly, the Apollo Program had barely begun when tragedy struck the space program and the nation. On the ground at a building in Florida, astronauts Gus Grissom, Roger Chaffee, and Ed White were strapped into the cabin of an Apollo spacecraft and the doors were sealed for a standard preflight test.

Suddenly a spark ignited the oxygen-rich air inside. The men never had a chance. All three lost their lives. They were burned to death before anyone could open the hatch.

Michael was in a meeting with Apollo director Alan Shepard when the phone rang with the terrible news. The astronauts rallied around one another. It fell to Michael to go to Chaffee's house nearby and deliver the news to Martha Chaffee, Roger's wife, before she heard it on television or elsewhere.

Grissom and Chaffee were buried at Arlington National Cemetery outside Washington, DC. Michael was there in his air force uniform along with other astronauts. White's funeral was at the same time but at West Point, where he and Collins had studied together.

The shocking deaths might have ended Apollo. But the astronauts and their families chose to carry on. They understood that there was danger, but they didn't quit. For their part, Michael and his wife, Pat, rarely spoke of the risk. They just did the job.

Later that year Michael and Pat traveled to France, where Michael represented NASA at the Paris Air Show. There he met with Russian pilots and astronauts. At that time the US and Russia were deadly enemies. They were engaged in the Cold War and the space race. But Michael treated the Soviets as fellow pilots, not as enemies. They compared planes they'd flown and talked about what it was like to go to space. By this time, eleven Soviet astronauts, known as cosmonauts, had reached space. (Among that group was Valentina Tereshkova, the first woman in space.) Michael knew he could not end the Cold War just by talking shop, but he appreciated the chance to meet fellow spacemen and airmen.

The Cold War

In 1945, World War II ended, but another kind of conflict began. The Cold War was between the Soviet Union (USSR) and the United States. Following World War II, the Soviet Union greatly expanded its territory. And it wanted even more around the world. The United States pushed back strongly. These battles weren't fought with tanks and planes but with spies, words, and money.

During the Cold War, a physical wall was built to divide the city of Berlin, Germany, into east and west. The country of Germany was also divided, politically, into east and west. Numerous nations in Eastern Europe were taken over by the USSR. Meanwhile, the United States worked to prevent even further Soviet spread in Africa, South America, and Asia. The Soviet Union was Communist, while Germany and the United States were democracies.

Looming over everyone in all of this was the fact that both the United States and the Soviet Union had nuclear weapons. None were ever used, which is why the war was "cold." But the threat made those days very warm indeed. In 1989 the wall between

East Berlin and West Berlin fell, and by 1991 the Soviet Union had broken up. The Cold War was finally over.

Michael and Pat enjoyed a final treat in Europe. They were surprised to be invited to renew their wedding vows in a small chapel in Metz, France. They had married there in 1957 when he was stationed in Europe with the air force. The joy of the wedding vows helped restore some happiness to their lives, which had been so recently touched by tragedy.

14.
PREPARING FOR
THE MOON

Michael almost had to leave the Apollo Program himself, though not because of an accident. In 1968 he had serious neck surgery. He had developed a problem with two bones in his spine. He needed an operation to fix it. He was in pain and was having trouble moving. The operation would probably fix things, but he was worried for a while that he would not be able to return to his astronaut work. For three months he had to wear a metal brace that held his neck perfectly still. At times he had on a body cast that stretched from his waist to the back of his head. But the operation turned out perfectly, and he was able to get back to work. He was frustrated, however, for one of the few times in his life. During the time when he wasn't working, other crews were set up. The flight he had been assigned to, now called *Apollo 8*, had a new crew. It would be flying around the moon, while he was stuck back on Earth because of his operation. But once again he put aside his personal feelings and carried on with the mission.

Michael's new role for the *Apollo 8* mission was as CapCom. That stood for "capsule communicator." (Yes, it uses that word "capsule.") The CapCom was the person—almost always a fellow astronaut—who spoke to the astronaut crew and relayed information. The crew asked him questions, and he found answers. Having only one voice for this communication made sure that the information was always received and was always accurate. Also, NASA saw it as a benefit to have an astronaut CapCom talking to astronaut crew members. Astronauts understood all the same terms and words. They could speak the same technical language. For the *Apollo 8* mission three astronauts took turns being the CapCom, but Michael went first, so he was CapCom during the launch.

Up until this point, there had only been one manned Apollo flight, *Apollo 7*. The crew that had died had been given the special mission name *Apollo 1*. Five other missions had just tested spacecraft and had been unmanned. Three astronauts on *Apollo 7* had flown around Earth for eleven days, testing many systems.

Apollo 8, however, would be the first time that human beings would fly around the moon.

On launch day, December 21, 1968, Michael talked the crew through each step of their work as the rocket rose from the pad. It was a nervous time. Any launch is tricky, but the Saturn V rocket that *Apollo 8* used was still fairly new. It would have been Michael's job to tell the men to bail out if something went wrong.

Apollo 8 had a second rocket on board. After the crew was in orbit around Earth, the second rocket would ignite and send them toward the moon. This was a huge step, almost as big as the one Armstrong would make the following year while Michael flew above him. For the first time human beings would break out of Earth's orbit and fly to the moon. There they would enter orbit around our closest space neighbor.

Michael later wrote that the three astronauts, once they left our orbit, "would have to be counted apart from all the other billions."[9] He didn't know at the time that he would soon be even more apart.

As Michael worked day by day with *Apollo 8*, the crew on the spaceship was seeing Earth from far above. It was something no one had ever done before. One of the color pictures they took was called *Earthrise*. It showed our home planet rising above the edge of the moon just as we see the sun or moon rising above our horizon. It was a stunning photo. Billions of people saw their home in a brand-new way. The worldwide environmental movement, which had started slowly in the 1960s, got a huge boost. All of a sudden here was a photo that showed that all of us on the planet actually did share a single home. We are not only a mix of countries and cities. We are a single, unified planet in the solar system. And seeing our blue-and-green home so tiny in enormous space made many realize that we have to take better care of it.

The *Apollo 8* crew also took the first close-up pictures of the surface of the moon. Bill Anders, one of the crew, said that he thought the dusty, crater-filled land was black and unappealing. They also experienced an odd sensation. During their orbits around the moon, they "disappeared." When they were above the side of the moon that always faces away from Earth, no one could hear them. The radio signals could not reach Earth; it was called "loss of signal." For more than forty minutes, the *Apollo 8* crew vanished from NASA's radar and radio signals. It was a very nervous time. If something happened to them, NASA might never know what went wrong. Then the radio crackled as they swung back around, safe and sound. This loss of signal was something that Michael would also experience, but with one important difference: he would be completely alone.

After twenty orbits, the crew fired the thrusters that blasted them out of the moon's gravity, and they began the long journey home.

Michael's next big job came a couple of days later. Just as *Apollo 8* had been the first spacecraft to orbit the moon, it would also be the first to have to travel back to Earth. Falling into Earth's atmosphere from *Earth's* orbit is tricky. Falling from a distance many times higher than that was trickier . . . and more dangerous. The crew had one shot to enter the atmosphere at the correct angle. It was part of Michael's job to help them.

It worked perfectly! The spacecraft blasted through the atmosphere in the right place and at the right speed. It landed in the ocean near a US Navy ship. Michael had had a very trying time, but he had made important contributions to another successful mission.

A few weeks later, in early 1969, Michael got some news that would change his life. NASA announced the crew of *Apollo 11*. This was the mission that was, at that moment, scheduled to land on the moon. *Apollo 11*'s crew would be Neil Armstrong, commander; Edwin "Buzz" Aldrin, lunar module pilot; and Michael Collins, command module pilot.

Two of those men would actually set foot on the moon, the first men ever to do so. The third man would not.

Michael Collins was that third man.

15.
PATCHES AND PACKING

The *Apollo 11* flight was scheduled for mid-July 1969, so the men had a lot of work to do in a short time. Michael spent a lot of that time back in a simulator. He was continuing to learn all he could about the command module (CM). That was the part of the Apollo craft that would stay in orbit around the moon. The lunar module (LM) would separate and land on the moon. After a few hours on the moon, the LM would fly back, and the two modules would join up again. The three astronauts would fly home together in the CM.

In the simulator, Michael practiced linking up with the LM. He went over all the things to do while the others were on the moon. And he repeatedly worked on the skills needed to bring the crew all safely back to Earth.

Others were also practicing, but they worked in space. The *Apollo 9* mission blasted off in March. It was the first to have the CM and LM separate and then rejoin in space. It was a vital test. If it had not worked, *Apollo 11* would not have flown. Though *Apollo 9* did not land on the moon, the crew also tested the space suits that Armstrong and Aldrin would use there. Astronaut Russell Schweickart did an EVA wearing a moon suit. It worked perfectly.

While Michael learned his new skills, he was also gathering a collection of odd little items. Each Apollo astronaut was allowed a "personal preference kit." This small bag could be carried into space with whatever the astronaut wanted. Most took a variety of items they could later give to friends and family.

They could say the gift had "been to space." Michael had his own set of pins, badges, coins, and similar tokens. People working for NASA as well as friends asked him to carry things for them. He couldn't take them all, but he knew how much these would mean to people, so he carried what he could.

He also took on an unusual duty: designing the mission logo. Today there would probably be a design company in charge. Or a national contest. Or NASA would take charge. For the Apollo flights, though, the crew had a big say in it. The three men decided they would not include their own names, as the other Apollo mission logos had done. This was important. They believed they were representing all of humanity, not just themselves. Michael came up with the idea of an eagle landing on the moon, to symbolize America's role. A NASA employee thought of putting an olive branch with the eagle. The olive branch is a symbol for peace. But being a pilot, Michael did not want to put the branch in the eagle's claws. How would the bird land? In the end Michael didn't get his way, and the final design showed the huge bird holding a green-and-brown branch.

Because of the logo design, the LM soon got the name of *Eagle*. Michael's CM was named *Columbia*. That's a word based on the name of Christopher Columbus, who was supposed to have "discovered" America. By then people knew that he hadn't, but the name "Columbia" had long been connected to America. (Bonus fact: The *Apollo 10* spacecraft had funnier names. The CM was called *Charlie Brown*, after the Peanuts comic strip character. The LM? *Snoopy*, of course!)

The importance of the *Apollo 11* mission also called for some other ideas. The astronauts would plant an American flag, but what else could they leave? A big part of the LM would remain on the moon's surface. So NASA attached a small disk, much like a modern CD, to one leg of the LM. There were notes from presidents and kings and prime ministers from around the world on the disk.

While all this preparation was going on, Michael was writing a book. It ended up having 117 pages and one topic: what to do while he was all alone in the CM. He called it a *Solo Book*. He had hundreds of switches to operate and dials and gauges to watch. He had to communicate with NASA and the men on the moon. He had to watch his orbital path carefully. And he had to be ready for any emergency. In fact, he came up with eighteen different ways that the LM might have trouble reaching the CM. Michael wanted to be ready for anything.

When the LM left Michael and the CM, he would be completely alone on a spacecraft whizzing around the moon. He would have no other astronauts to help him. For a long time he would not even be able to use the radio, as *Apollo 8* had found.

Walking on the moon was an incredible challenge, of course, but Michael's part of the mission might have been harder. For instance, there was a chance that he would have to leave the others on the moon and fly home alone if they could not lift off in the LM. The CM could not land and get Armstrong and Aldrin; that was impossible. In the simulator Michael had to practice flying back into Earth's atmosphere alone . . . just in case.

In mid-May, *Apollo 10* continued the testing in space. This time the crew practiced the CM-LM linkup around the moon itself. They had to make sure their machines would work in lunar orbit. Once again, all systems were go! *Apollo 10* returned safely.

About a month before *Apollo 11* would take off, the three men moved into special crew quarters at Cape Kennedy in Florida. (The name had been changed from Cape Canaveral in 1963 following the death of President Kennedy.) They had a lot to do, so they wanted to be near their working areas. They also wanted to make sure that they were healthy for the flight, so they avoided people who might spread germs. (They even had to turn down dinner with President Richard Nixon for that reason.)

Michael wrote later that as the flight neared, he "really felt . . . pressure, this awesome sense of responsibility weighing" him down.[10]

He got some help from home. His wife, Pat, wrote him a note to read shortly before the launch. It included a poem in which she sent her love and encouragement to Michael. [Note: You can find the poem online in several places.]

Over the next few days the crew of *Apollo 11* would need their courage. But they were ready for anything that might head their way.

16.
LIFTOFF!

People lined the hallway as the three men walked by. The crew could not hear anything outside their helmets, however. Their suits were already sealed, and they carried small packs that pumped in oxygen.

They got into a van that would drive them past photographers and TV cameras to the launchpad.

Michael was carrying a very unusual package. Astronauts have many traditions. One of them is to give the man who runs the launchpad a present before the crew rises to the top of the rocket. Michael knew that this man, Guenter Wendt, loved to fish. So to tease him, Michael had a very tiny fish put on a plaque with the words "Guenter's Trophy Trout."[11] It gave them a final minute to smile before the serious work of the day continued.

Michael climbed into the cockpit second, after Armstrong. He took the seat on the right-hand side. Then Aldrin climbed into the middle. After a few final checks, the hatch was closed. The astronauts were alone.

But they were busy. The three men worked with NASA control and CapCom to go over several checklists to make sure everything was ready for flight. Armstrong checked to make sure he could reach a handle next to his leg. In an emergency during launch, he could pull it to eject the command module, which could then parachute to Earth. But that was possible for only the first three minutes of the flight. After that point there was no turning back.

Finally the countdown began. Millions of people

were watching on TV while thousands more aimed binoculars and cameras from the land around Cape Canaveral.

Five . . .

Four . . .

Three . . .

Two . . .

One . . .

Ignition! The enormous rocket engine fired, and smoke and flames poured from the bottom of the Saturn V launch vehicle.

Liftoff! The thirty-six-story-tall machine rose from the ground. It moved slowly at first but picked up speed almost instantly. The three men went from zero feet per second to more than nine thousand feet per second!

Atop the huge rocket, Armstrong, Aldrin, and Michael were shaking violently, but their straps held them in place. They did not talk; it was too loud, and there was not much to say.

For more than ten minutes they rocketed upward. Two different pieces of the rocket finished their work and fell away.

After a few more minutes they had reached space. The men felt weightlessness. Michael peered out again at the view from space that he had loved seeing in *Gemini 10*. The men could take off their helmets and gloves, because the cabin had oxygen for them to breathe. Of course, without gravity, things were starting to float around too. Michael had to ask for help finding a camera that had drifted away from him.

The men made sure that everything was working well in the spacecraft. They admired the amazing view and took photos and movies.

17.
A THREE-DAY TRIP

Soon *Apollo 11* was ready to leave orbit. Following instructions from NASA, they ignited the final part of the Saturn V rocket, which blasted the spacecraft to more than thirty-five thousand miles per hour. Slowly the three astronauts felt Earth's gravity slip away. They were on their way to the moon!

Michael's first big job was to set up the command module (CM) and the lunar module (LM) for this trip. When everything was ready, he pushed a button, and the CM disconnected from the rocket holding the LM. Then very, very carefully he spun the CM around in a half circle, and inch by inch, while soaring at high speed toward the moon, he would connect them again. The reason? It hadn't been possible to have the two modules connected inside the rocket. This new connection set them up perfectly to go to and from the moon.

Michael watched on a screen as the crosshairs of a big X appeared atop the LM. He guided the CM with tiny movements using his hand controls. Armstrong and Aldrin helped by watching through windows, but this was Michael's job. The two modules got closer and closer until . . . contact!

A final burst of a thruster moved the twin craft away from what was left of the rocket. The mighty Saturn V had done its job. It would now continue its journey through space for weeks until finally burning up in the sun.

The men adjusted thrusters to keep the spacecraft spinning very slowly. This was to prevent one side of the craft from facing the sun all the time. That would make it—and them—too hot.

Finally, after all their chores were done—and their bulky space suits were stored away—it was time for sleep.

For the next three days they took care of the spacecraft, completing chore after chore. They took photos and talked to people on Earth. At one point the men filmed a short movie that was beamed back to Earth. They ate, of course. Their food included salmon, chicken soup, salad, peanut cubes, and water and coffee. Michael even tried to get in a "run." He held on to the side of the craft and pushed his legs around as if he were running in place.

On the fourth day the men finally arrived at the moon. It loomed large in their windows.

The crew worked with Houston to fire thrusters that put them into orbit around the moon itself. For several orbits the trio looked out the windows and marveled at what they were seeing. They snapped pictures as Earth "rose" behind the moon. At one point Michael took a photo of a particular crater on the moon's surface. He gave it a name: KAMP. That stood for "Kate, Ann, Michael, and Patricia"—his family.

The astronauts went around and around, taking measurements and snapping pictures. They paid careful attention to the area near the Sea of Tranquility. There are no real seas on the moon. However, astronomers use the word "sea" to mean a large, flat area on the moon. "Tranquility" means "peacefulness." The mission specialists had chosen to have the LM land on what they hoped would be a safe, flat spot without too many craters. From high above the moon the men of *Apollo 11* looked at crater after crater but decided that the landing spot looked good.

Soon they got to sleep again. All three had trouble getting much rest. They knew what was ahead. The next day was July 20—the day men would finally walk on the moon.

18.
ON THE MOON

After waking up on July 20, the three astronauts prepared for the big moment. Michael helped the other two put on their full pressure suits, including helmets and gloves. Armstrong and Aldrin floated into the LM, while Michael stayed in the CM getting ready for the separation of the LM.

As Michael watched them go, he sincerely hoped he would see them again.

The hatch between the two machines was shut, and at a signal from the LM, Michael flipped a switch. The clawlike clamps released, and a little push from a tiny thruster sent the two machines apart. "The *Eagle* has wings," said Neil Armstrong.[12]

"You guys take care," Collins said over the radio.

"See you later," Armstrong said in his usual quiet way.[13]

Not long after, as more than half a billion people around the world—and one around the moon—listened in, *Eagle* slowly headed toward the surface. Michael could not see them far below. He sometimes could not even hear them. He often could only hear NASA back on Earth. They relayed news to him.

Armstrong and Aldrin guided *Eagle* carefully toward the landing site. At the last minute Armstrong took control away from the computers. He had spotted a large boulder in the direct path of the landing craft. There was no time for another try. They had to land right then or risk running out of fuel. After a decade of planning and millions of hours of meetings, the final yards of travel to the moon were in the hands of one man. Ever the expert pilot, Armstrong calmly redirected the craft to avoid the boulder. For man's first landing on the moon, it was a man who did the landing . . . not a computer. He found just the right spot and put *Eagle* down.

"Houston," Armstrong called over the radio, "Tranquility Base [the code name for the landing site] here. The *Eagle* has landed."

"Fantastic!" Michael yelled when he got the news. The first and perhaps most dangerous step was safely done. *Eagle* had landed on the moon![14]

Later Armstrong would radio up to Michael, "Just keep that orbiting base ready for us up there now."

Armstrong and Aldrin stepped onto the surface about six hours later, after running numerous safety tests. "That's one small step for a man, one giant leap for mankind," Armstrong said as he put the first human footprint in the dust of the moon. They spent two and a half hours on the surface gathering rocks and taking pictures. Then they climbed back into *Eagle* for some much-deserved rest.

19.
ALONE

Meanwhile, Michael whirled around the moon. Remember "loss of signal" (LOS)? From now on he would experience that eerie quiet all alone.

As he entered LOS over and over, each time he was the most isolated person in human history. He was completely separate from Earth and every person on it. He could not even connect with his crewmates on the moon. Imagine how that must have felt! A person in a dark coal mine is closer to other human contact than Michael was for those periods during LOS.[15]

NASA said of his position, "Not since Adam [who, according to the Bible, was the first human] has any human known such solitude as Michael Collins is experiencing" during LOS.

"I am alone . . . truly alone," Michael later wrote, "and absolutely isolated from any known life. I am it."[16] Yet Michael said he did not mind. As a pilot he was used to flying alone, high above the ground. (Though, he had never flown *this* high, of course.) "The idea of being in a flying vehicle alone was in no way alarming. In fact, sometimes I prefer to be by myself."[17]

Michael, like most astronauts, did not spend a lot of time worrying. He just did his job. He realized how important it was, and he knew they were making history. But in the moment he did not think, *My gosh, I'm incredibly scared to be alone.* He just went through his checklists and waited patiently until he got Houston on the radio again.

He certainly was not bored. In the final part of

his journey alone, he had to push different computer buttons a total of eight hundred fifty times. Each one had to be pushed at the right moment in the right order, or who knows what might have gone wrong. He had to have very fierce concentration. There was too much at stake for him to worry about being alone.

He was up there for twenty-eight hours, going round and round the moon. Michael was seventy miles above the lunar surface and every two hours "disappeared" from Earth. While he was back there, he noticed that he could not see the moon. It was blocking all the sunlight, so there was nothing shining on the side of the moon he faced. Michael could only "see" the moon as the black circle where he could see no stars.

At one point when Armstrong and Aldrin were on the moon, NASA pointed out that Michael was probably the only person who could not see them on TV. The landing was televised live to billions of people worldwide, but not to the *Columbia* spacecraft.

Later he would write of his time alone, "Far from feeling lonely or abandoned, I feel very much a part of what is taking place on the lunar surface. . . . This venture has been structured for three men, and I consider my third to be as necessary as either of the other two."[18]

And, amazingly, for part of his time alone, he took a nap.

20.
THE MOST IMPORTANT JOB OF ALL

While Michael did not worry about himself while he was alone, he was concerned about one important job ahead. He had to do everything just right so that he would be in the correct place to meet the LM and get Armstrong and Aldrin back on board the CM. If something went wrong, he might have to leave his fellow astronauts on the moon. For years after his flight Michael was asked whether he, Armstrong, and Aldrin had talked about that terrible possibility. He usually said that they just didn't talk about it. Everyone knew what the job was. They couldn't change anything by talking about it.

Still, as the moment arrived far, far above Earth, Michael himself knew what could happen. "I have never sweated out any flight like I am sweating out the [arrival of the] LM now. My secret terror for the last six months has been leaving them on the moon and returning to Earth alone."[19]

Once the time for the LM to launch from the moon was set, there was a key problem to solve. It had not landed exactly where they had planned, so Michael had to find it. He never did see it from orbit. And if he didn't know where it was, he could not meet up with it.

Then there was the issue of the LM rocket. It had never fired in space before. If it did not work, there was no way for Armstrong and Aldrin to escape from the moon. The two astronauts would be stuck, and there would be nothing Michael or anyone else could do.

As the preparation for the liftoff from the moon began, Armstrong managed a pilot joke. "We're number one on the runway," he said.

After a short countdown, the button was pushed . . . and the rocket worked! *Eagle* rose, leaving behind the bottom half of the LM, including the legs, on the moon. Those spacecraft parts are still sitting up there in the dust fifty years later.

Michael was overjoyed to hear that his friends were rising to safety. "I got really excited then because for the first time it was clear they had done it. They had landed on the moon and got off again."[20]

Michael then guided *Columbia* once more around the moon. The computers would guide the two spacecraft toward the same orbit. Then the two pilots would use their skill and training to connect the two modules.

As he came around the moon, Michael was finally able to see *Eagle*. He managed to take an amazing photo of the LM rising toward him. Behind it was the moon. And behind the moon, in the distance, was Earth. Later he would realize that in that photo was every living thing in the history of Earth, alive or dead . . . except him.

As the two craft got nearer and nearer, Michael and Armstrong talked constantly. Each made tiny adjustments to line up the two craft. Finally it was up to Michael to make the grab. Just a moment before he was ready to go, something went slightly wrong. Both craft began to wobble a bit. Michael later wrote that *Eagle* was acting like a "wildly veering critter." But it was not as bad as that. Just a few seconds later both pilots had lined up again.[21]

A moment later they were locked together. Michael breathed a huge sigh of relief. It was done.

The two moon walkers floated through the tunnel between the CM and the LM. They shook hands with Michael. Then they passed boxes of rocks to Michael to stow away. "I was glad to see [Neil and Buzz]," he wrote in *Life* magazine. "They allowed as how they were happy to be back."[22]

Thanks from Home

While the astronauts were heading home, they were given many messages of congratulations. One in particular caught Michael's attention. Mrs. Esther Goddard had written to say how thrilled she was at their success. Her husband, Robert Goddard, had been the American scientist who in the 1920s had helped invent rocketry. Without his work, there might not have been an Apollo Program.

During his early days of invention, Goddard had gotten help and money from the Smithsonian Institution. Later Michael would become a director at the Smithsonian. Some journeys just go around in circles.

21.
COMING HOME, PART 2

After a few more orbits around the moon, *Columbia* was ready to start the trip home. The crew worked with NASA to fire the ship's thrusters at just the right moment. That blasted them out of the moon's orbit and toward Earth. They had to be precise, or else they might fly right by their home planet.

But it was a perfect "burn," as the astronauts call these short bursts of fuel. For the next two and a half days, they were tourists in space. There were no experiments and only a few duties to keep them busy.

They did take time to make a short movie for children on Earth, showing life in zero gravity. Michael demonstrated how he "drank" water from a spoon . . . even if the spoon was upside down!

The men also recorded their final thoughts for the TV camera. All three made sure to thank the many, many people who had helped make their trip possible. Michael talked about the difficulties and the dangers and how proud he was of being a part of something that had been so hard but had gone so well. Aldrin talked more about the meaning of the trip, as the first part of a journey to space that he hoped would continue for a long time into the future. Armstrong thanked the workers, and also the American people for paying for the whole thing!

As the spacecraft finally approached Earth, Michael was in the all-important pilot seat on the left side of the cabin.

He had to ensure that *Columbia* was at the correct angle to enter the atmosphere. If not, they would skip on the air. Or they might enter too steeply and get too hot. But Michael nailed it.

The bottom of the craft was covered by a heat shield. As Michael had done during his Gemini flight, he watched out the window as the burning shield made a brilliant light show. He saw reds and yellows, but also blues, purples, and greens. Finally Aldrin announced that the first two parachutes had popped out. A few moments later the three main chutes came out. "They are a sight to behold!" Michael wrote.[23] In a 2017 interview he joked that seeing those chutes open was his most memorable moment of the entire trip!

Down the CM floated until they hit the water in the Pacific Ocean with a huge splash. Once again the navy was on the spot, and divers quickly secured *Columbia*. When the hatch opened, the divers threw in special coveralls. All three astronauts had to wear them.

Then the astronauts climbed into floating baskets and were hoisted up into the helicopter overhead.

After the helicopter landed on the navy recovery

ship, the astronauts walked directly into what looked like a huge metal sausage to begin the quarantine process. The men were home, after nine days. But it would be almost three weeks before they could hug their kids.

One of the things that most worried NASA was that Armstrong and Aldrin would bring back some new kind of germ from the moon. No one knew if there were things on the moon that could harm humans. Of course, once Armstrong and Aldrin had moved into the CM again, Michael had been exposed to the same things. (Both of the moon walkers were covered in moondust when they went aboard the CM, for instance.) So the men went from one sort of confined space to another. All three were put into the quarantine trailer, which was a huge pressurized box. Two other NASA workers were already inside to help the men, and to make *Columbia* itself safe for travel. It was also connected to the quarantine sausage.

The men were very happy to get out of their

smelly space suits. Remember, there are no showers or bathtubs in space. Just about every astronaut talks about the horrible smell in the enclosed cabin after a long time has passed! After they cleaned up, they got a surprise: President Nixon was waiting outside the quarantine facility to congratulate them on their success. He spoke through a microphone and thanked them again for their great work.

The men then enjoyed a steak dinner and the USS *Hornet* sailed to Pearl Harbor in Hawaii. (Before then, though, Michael made a final mark on *Columbia*. He took a pen and wrote the date and his name on the inside of the ship he had spent so much time in. "The best ship to come down the line," he wrote.)[24]

The trailer they were in went through a parade in Honolulu with thousands of people waving in the streets. From there the entire quarantine trailer was flown to Houston. Finally, at a short ceremony the men got to see their wives. They could only talk to them through a telephone, though. The hugs would have to wait.

The unit was moved into a sealed building. Collins, Armstrong, and Aldrin had to stay inside with the NASA workers and other helpers for more than two weeks to make sure they did not get sick. NASA didn't want any germs that the astronauts might have to spread to other humans. Inside the box they could clean up, eat, sleep, and simply wait. They could talk to people and peer out windows to see their families. But they could not be allowed to touch people yet, just to make sure the astronauts were safe and hadn't brought back anything. (Also in the box and the building were some mice. If the mice started to get sick or die after being near the astronauts, that would have been a signal that something was wrong. "We were really glad to hear that the mice stayed healthy and didn't pick up any moon bugs," Michael wrote later.[25])

The astronauts' time in the giant sealed building was not a total vacation. They worked hard every day.

There were reports to write about the trip, and many scientists wanted to talk to them through the window speakers. Fellow astronauts came to learn all they could. At least six more Apollo missions to the moon were scheduled at that point, and the members of this crew were now the only world experts on the trip. They also caught up on the news they'd missed, and read lots of letters and telegrams praising their deeds.

Eventually the doctors at NASA cleared the men. They were let out of the box . . . and then the party started.

Letter from Another "Man Alone"

While in quarantine, Michael got one letter he was especially proud to receive. It was from Charles Lindbergh, the first person to fly nonstop across the Atlantic Ocean. His 1927 flight was perhaps the most famous air trip before *Apollo 11*. Lindbergh, too, became an international celebrity. He praised Michael for his piloting skill. He also shared his wonder of what it must have been like for Michael to be by himself, just as Lindbergh had been during his flight in 1927. "You have experienced an aloneness unknown to man before," the famous pilot wrote. "I felt closer to you in orbit than to your fellow astronauts."[26]

22.
AROUND THE WORLD AGAIN

America wanted to celebrate its new heroes, so the astronauts were taken to a very narrow, famous street in New York City. Known as the Canyon of Heroes, it's located on lower Broadway, and tall buildings loom over it on both sides. For decades the city had greeted heroes with special parades. From the windows of the buildings, workers showered the heroes with paper. In the early days the paper was long, thin rolls that came out of a ticker-tape machine, which showed stock prices. By 1969 ticker tape had been joined by confetti and just about any other kind of paper.

On August 13 the men rode sitting in the back of a convertible. More than two million people lined the street to wave at and see the famous explorers. Usually such parades only go for a few blocks, but for this one, organizers went all out. The route headed from the bottom of Broadway all the way to Times Square. "It's wonderful. It's exciting. The best part of all is being here," Armstrong said.[27]

The parade continued to the United Nations building, where they were greeted by Secretary-General U Thant.

But all that was only the beginning of a *loooong* day. The astronauts and their wives then flew to Chicago for another packed parade. Then they took a longer flight to Los Angeles. There President Nixon hosted them and all fifty US governors, along with hundreds of special guests and celebrities. He had invited them to the event, which was held in their honor, during his visit on the USS *Hornet*. He promised the astronauts they would not have to make long speeches.

If they had thought that their long travels were over, they were wrong.

All three *Apollo 11* astronauts had circled Earth, on this spaceflight and on earlier missions. After returning from the moon, they circled it again . . . in a very different way. President Nixon wanted to show off America's success. He sent the three astronauts and their wives on a long, tiring, amazing, colorful journey. They flew around the world on what was called, after what Armstrong had said on the moon, the Giant Leap tour.

In thirty-eight days they visited twenty-three countries. They were seen by millions of people on three continents. They met kings, queens, presidents, and even the pope. The trip started in Mexico City. The astronauts put on huge sombreros and were given yet another parade watched by millions. They then traveled through South America and across the

Atlantic Ocean to Europe. After stopping in Spain, France, the Netherlands, Belgium, Norway, Germany, and England, the group had a special audience (or meeting) with Pope Paul VI in Vatican City. After that the entire group got some much-needed rest. They stayed at the American embassy in Rome for a little taste of home. They swam in the pool and had barbecued hamburgers and hot dogs.

In Yugoslavia the wives got a ride on a superfast riverboat while the men toured the countryside in a bus. Then it was off to Turkey and Africa. At one stop in Zaire, the group was entertained by African dancers.

"I remember Buzz Aldrin [leaped] over the guard rail where the astronauts were seated and started dancing with members of the group. Quite a crowd pleaser," said Geneva Barnes. She worked for NASA and had helped plan the Giant Leap tour, only to find out that she would be going on the entire journey herself too.[28]

Sometimes the crowds were too much. At one stop in Pakistan the people surged past the guards. They surrounded the cars carrying the astronauts so tightly that the vehicles could barely move. In Iran the group got to visit an underground vault that held the fabulous crown jewels of the shah.

The last leg of the trip took them to Asia, including stops in Japan and South Korea. Then they flew back across the Pacific and America to Washington, DC, to wrap up this very different kind of orbit.

Armstrong and Aldrin were the most famous men in the world. They had walked on the moon! Everyone wanted to see them and cheer for them. Michael got cheers, too, but not as loud. The three men did everything together, but most people wanted to hear from the men who'd been on the moon, not the man who'd been in the spacecraft. When people did ask him questions, they almost always asked what it had been like *not* to step on the moon or what it had been like to be so alone.

Michael didn't really mind the questions at first. He was pleased that the mission had been a success. He knew he had done his part.

What Michael had not told his crewmates, though he had told his wife, Pat, was that *Apollo 11* had been his last time in space. NASA was probably going to offer him another flight, one that might give him time on the moon. He probably could have commanded *Apollo 17*, set to launch in 1972.

But he had decided weeks before *Apollo 11* that if the mission was a success, he was done. He had spent enough time away from Pat and his children, he felt. He had accomplished all the jobs he had been given. His duty was done.

23.
HIS NEXT BIG JOB

It turned out that Michael's Earth-bound trip around the world was a perfect setup for his next job. In January 1970 he was named the assistant secretary of state for public affairs. He would work in the State Department, the part of the American government that communicates with other nations. But rather than traveling to other countries, Michael spoke with the public and the media in the United States, to explain and spread the word about how Americans connected to the rest of the world. The State

Department called him their "supersalesman."[29] He visited schools around the United States, spoke at conferences, and traveled almost as often as he had in the space program.

In 1971, Michael got the chance to make another important mark on the world. He was named director of the National Air and Space Museum, part of the Smithsonian Institution in Washington, DC. His main role would be to make sure a new, expanded museum building would be finished by 1976. Why that year? The United States celebrated its two hundredth birthday in 1976, and the Smithsonian wanted to make a big splash.

Running the museum and the construction project was a lot like working at NASA—there were lots and lots of people all doing their own jobs that together made something really big. Of course, for Michael, working at a museum celebrating flight and space travel was a dream come true. He spent his time around things that he later said were old friends of his. He saw his spaceship *Columbia* installed in the front of the museum itself.

The National Air and Space Museum

Today the National Air and Space Museum is one of the most popular sites in Washington, DC. It's filled with tens of thousands of objects from hundreds of years of flight. Visitors see original NASA vehicles, the Wright brothers' airplane, moon rocks, other famous airplanes, and much more.

The collection of those objects started long before there was a special museum devoted to aviation. In the 1870s the Smithsonian Institution started gathering hot-air balloons and other items from early flight. Interest in aviation leaped after the Wright brothers' airplane flight in 1903, and more and more machines and objects joined the Smithsonian collection.

In 1946, President Harry Truman helped establish a museum specifically for these aviation artifacts. It was called the National Air Museum, and the collection continued to grow, filling several buildings around Washington, DC, and even in other states. In 1966 the name of the museum was changed to the National Air and Space Museum, to acknowledge that the technology for flight was continuing to advance–into space.

In 1971, following the success of the Apollo Program, the Smithsonian finally decided to put its huge air and space collection into one place. A new building was planned on the National Mall, near the Washington Monument. Under the direction of Michael Collins, the new building opened on July 1, 1976. Within six months of the new museum's opening, five million people had visited. The parade of curious air and space lovers continues. More than eight million people now visit each year. It is the most popular museum in the United States.

In 2003 a companion air and space museum opened in Virginia. The Udvar-Hazy Center holds the enormous airplanes, rockets, and other giant machines that won't fit into the building in Washington, DC.

Just as he had while preparing for the moon trip, Michael made lists and checked things off. He ran a team of people that worked hard, and he was at the center of the action. He had become good at speaking to large groups and "selling" the museum.

Finally, on July 1, 1976, it was mission accomplished! With President Gerald Ford watching, among many other famous people, a ribbon was cut to open the amazing new museum. They didn't use scissors, however. A robot with a cutting blade received a signal from a far-off NASA space probe called *Viking 1* to snip at just the right moment.

Michael later said that he was especially proud of what the museum could do for the future. "Buildings like this do a lot to sustain that level of interest [in the space program]," he said.[30]

During his time at the Smithsonian, Michael was busy after work. In 1974 a long book was published about his entire flying career. *Carrying the Fire: An Astronaut's Journeys* got great reviews. Some still think it is the best-written story by anyone who has been to space. In 1976 he wrote the same story for younger audiences, in *Flying to the Moon*. In the book you're reading now, many of the words from Michael came from those two books.

He also went back to school. He studied at Harvard University to get an advanced degree in business. When he left the Air and Space Museum in 1978, he put his new education to work. (He also retired from the air force in 1982, after thirty years. His final rank was major general.) Michael worked for LTV Aerospace and Defense Company, which was involved in space and aviation. In 1985 he started his own company. People, companies, and governments hired him to advise them on space travel, flying, and engineering.

In 1988 he wrote another book that told the whole story of America's space history, called *Liftoff: The Story of America's Adventure in Space*. He was able to comment on the space shuttle and other advances since his time in the Apollo Program.

24.
A PRIVATE LIFE . . . MOSTLY

As the world celebrates the fiftieth anniversary of the historic *Apollo 11* flight, its most "alone" astronaut spends most of his time alone at home now. His wife, Pat, passed away in 2014, and his children are grown with families of their own.

But Michael Collins remains busy. He often gives speeches or attends space events, such as the fortieth anniversary of *Apollo 11* in 2009. He visits universities to meet with engineering students—especially those who want to be involved in the space program—and has taken part in numerous events at the Smithsonian, his old home in Washington, DC.

Michael showed his love of writing with his three books. He also loves poetry and included some examples in his first book. When meeting with young people, he tells them it's certainly good to study STEM topics—science, technology, engineering, and math. But he prefers STEEM—the extra *E* is for "English." Michael believes that no matter what you do, you have to be able to express yourself well.

The man who once "ran" in space still stays in shape. He believes, and believed then, that it is very important to take care of our own human spacecraft. He told an interviewer that he tries to do one sprint triathlon a year—running, riding a bike, and swimming, one after the other.

Michael also paints. He has been making watercolors since the 1980s. While in space he discovered a deep love of the beauty of life on Earth. Many of his paintings are of animals or the land in the Florida

Everglades, near his home. He has also made paintings of some of the aircraft he has flown. Unlike some other astronauts-turned-artists, he has not created any paintings of space (that we know about). Like the humble person he is, he usually does not sign his work. When he does, he just prints "M. Collins." He doesn't want his paintings to be bought or sold just because they have his famous autograph.

The year 2019 marks fifty years since the men of *Apollo 11* made history. In the years since the moon landing, the space program has never really been as big as it was on that one day—July 20, 1969. Following the final Apollo mission—*Apollo 17* in 1972—NASA turned its attention to the space shuttle. These were airplane-like craft that flew from 1981 through 2011. Today the International Space Station is home to astronauts from several countries year-round. However, none of the launches of those people occurs in the United States. As of 2011 the spacecraft have all lifted off from bases in Russia.

MICHAEL COLLINS

In 2004, President George Bush said that the United States and the world should try to put a man on Mars. Others in the government said that the year 2030 would be the first goal. That call did not receive the support that Kennedy's had back in 1961. Work is proceeding on a manned mission to Mars, but only time will tell if it can happen.

For his part Michael is pretty certain that we'll get there someday. He has long spoken about the benefits of going to Mars, or even beyond to Titan, a moon of Jupiter.

He will watch our progress from behind his easel or walking through his garden. But every night he will be able to look up and see where he went.

"We earthlings are wanderers," he once said. "We always have been."[31]

If it is up to Michael Collins, we always will be.

Endnotes

1   Deep Space TV interview, Feb. 26, 2017.

2   Collins, Michael. *Carrying the Fire: An Astronaut's Journeys.* (New York: Farrar, Straus and Giroux, 1974), 92.

3   Collins, *Carrying the Fire*, 10.

4   Bryan Marquard, "Patricia Collins, 83; Wrote about Being an Astronaut's Wife," *The Boston Globe*, April 4, 2014. https://www.bostonglobe.com/metro/2014/05/03/patricia-collins-wrote-poignantly-about-being-astronaut-wife/tCrKU0SGaZoC7aO-Bo0tnWK/story.html

5   Collins, *Carrying the Fire*, 86.

6   Collins, *Carrying the Fire*, 183.

7   Collins, *Carrying the Fire*, 205.

8   Collins, *Carrying the Fire*, 223.

9   Collins, *Carrying the Fire*, 306.

10   Collins, *Carrying the Fire*, 349.

11   Collins, *Carrying the Fire*, 357.

12   Spacelog.org, http://apollo11.spacelog.org/page/04:04:18:04/

13   Spacelog.org, http://apollo11.spacelog.org/page/04:04:38:53/

14   James R. Hansen, *First Man: The Life of Neil A. Armstrong* (New York: Simon & Schuster, 2005), 277.

15   Space.com NASA log; https://www.space.com/26585-apollo-11-flight-log-july-21-1969.html

ENDNOTES

16 Collins, *Carrying the Fire*, 402.

17 Michael Collins, "The Astronauts—Their Own Great Stories," *Life* magazine, August 22, 1969, 27–29.

18 Collins, *Carrying the Fire*, 402.

19 Collins, *Carrying the Fire*, 411–12.

20 *Life* magazine, 28.

21 Collins, *Carrying the Fire*, 416.

22 *Life* magazine, 27.

23 Collins, *Carrying the Fire*, 440.

24 *Life* magazine, 29.

25 *Life* magazine, 27.

26 Collins, *Carrying the Fire*, 451.

27 *Desert Sun* newspaper, "Astronauts get first parade," from UPI, Aug. 13, 1969, 1.

28 NASA interview with Geneva Barnes, https://history.nasa.gov/SP-4223/ch10.htm

29 "Collins, Ex-Astronaut, on First State Trip." *The New York Times*, March 14, 1970. By Nan Robertson, 2.

30 Smithsonian YouTube interview, July 12, 2016. https://www.youtube.com/watch?v=1uODBHH9E90

31 Smithsonian YouTube interview.

Bibliography

Collins, Michael. *Carrying the Fire: An Astronaut's Journeys*. New York: Farrar, Straus and Giroux, 1974.

Collins, Michael. *Flying to the Moon: An Astronaut's Story*. 2nd ed. New York: Farrar, Straus and Giroux, 1994.

Collins, Michael. *Liftoff: The Story of America's Adventure in Space*. New York: Grove Press, 1988.

Hansen, James. R. *First Man: The Life of Neil A. Armstrong*. New York: Simon & Schuster, 2005.

Irvine, Alex. Ben Bishop, illus. *The Far Side of the Moon: The Story of Apollo 11's Third Man*. Thomaston, ME: Tilbury House, 2017.

Schyffert, Bea Uusma. *The Man Who Went to the Far Side of the Moon: The Story of Apollo 11 Astronaut Michael Collins*. San Francisco: Chronicle Books, 2003.

"The Astronauts—Their Own Great Stories." *Life* magazine, August 22, 1969, 22–29.

BIBLIOGRAPHY

"Air-to-Ground Transmission," Apollo XI, recorded by NASA—
https://www.hq.nasa.gov/alsj/a11/a11transcript_tec.html

Smithsonian interview with Collins, YouTube
https://www.youtube.com/watch?v=1uODBHH9E90

MIT Interview with Collins, YouTube
https://www.youtube.com/watch?v=ugNVvmmZuxg

STEM in 30 interview with Collins, YouTube
https://www.youtube.com/watch?v=8VXZDlsWxMQ

NASA interview with Collins, YouTube
https://www.youtube.com/watch?v=6HUeqkuGs7g

About the Author

JAMES BUCKLEY JR. has written more than 150 books for young readers, including many biographies. He has written fourteen books in the *New York Times* bestselling Who Was? series, including titles on the Wright brothers, Muhammad Ali, Milton Hershey, and Betsy Ross. He wrote four books in Penguin's Smithsonian space series for young readers, including an award-winning book on the International Space Station. He is also the coauthor of *X-Why-Z Space*, as well as the author of nature books such as *Snakeopedia* and *Bugopedia*. He lives in Santa Barbara, California, where he runs the Shoreline Publishing Group, a book producer.